SAS Platform Administrator for SAS9 (A00-250) Exam Practice Questions & Dumps

Exam Practice Questions for SAS A00-250
LATEST VERSION

Presented By: Quantic Books

About Quantic Books:

Quantic Books is a publishing house based in Princeton, New Jersey, USA. , a platform that is accessible online as well as locally, which gives power to educational content, erudite collection, poetry & many other book genres. We make it easy for writers & authors to get their books designed, published, promoted, and sell professionally on worldwide scale with eBook + Print distribution. Quantic Books is now distributing books worldwide.

Note: Find answers of the questions at the last of the book.

QUESTION 1

Which server does the Connection Profile allow you to connect to?

A. metadata server
B. workspace server
C. OLAP server
D. stored process server

QUESTION 2

In most deployments of the Platform for SAS Business Analytics, which type of access requires passwords for external accounts to be stored in the metadata?

A. seamless access to the SAS datasets
B. seamless access to SAS OLAP cubes
C. seamless access to external databases
D. all of the above

QUESTION 3

How do you modify the logging levels of a server without having to restart the server?

A. Modify the RollingFileAppender.
B. Use the IOM Server Appender to specify the message.
C. Use the Server Manager plug-in to modify the logger settings dynamically.
D. Modify the logconfig.xml file.

QUESTION 4

A platform administrator needs to update service account passwords in the metadata and configuration files. How can the platform administrator perform this configuration task?

A. Modify the RollingFileAppender.
B. Use the Server Manager plug-in.
C. Use the SAS Deployment Manager.
D. Modify the UpdatePasswords.html file.

QUESTION 5

Place the Log events in order of Diagnostic Level for severity from Highest (most severe) to Lowest.

A. DEBUG, INFO, ERROR, WARN
B. WARN, ERROR, DEBUG, TRACE
C. ERROR, DEBUG, TRACE, WARN
D. ERROR, WARN, INFO, DEBUG

QUESTION 6

Which process does NOT create a log file by default?

A. Metadata server
B. Workspace server
C. Object spawner
D. OLAP Server

QUESTION 7

A platform administrator is working with SAS OLAP servers and wants to: - display all OLAP servers and schemas - provide session controls - manage advanced server options How can the platform administrator perform these tasks?

A. open the Server Monitoring OLAP Tab
B. open the Server Monitoring Servers Tab
C. use the SAS OLAP Server Monitor plug-in
D. use the SAS Server Processes plug-in

QUESTION 8

A user needs to access data in a cube. The user has the following characteristics: Is in Enterprise Guide: OLAP role Does not have Read and ReadMetadata permissions for the cube What will be the result when the user attempts to access data in the cube?

A. The user will be able to access the data since Read and ReadMetadata permissions are not required.

B. The user will be able to access the data since they are using Enterprise Guide.

C. The user will be able to access the data since they are in the OLAP Role.

D. The user will not be able to access the data.

QUESTION 9

Which role is not pre-defined?

A. Enterprise Guide: Unrestricted
B. Enterprise Guide: Advanced
C. Enterprise Guide: Programming
D. Enterprise Guide: OLAP

QUESTION 10

The suffix of a SAS Internal account is:

A. @sas
B. @saspw
C. @LocalHost
D. @sasMain

QUESTION 11

Given the following authorization setup:

- Mary is a direct member of DeptA and DeptB

- Library Sales2 has an ACT denial for DeptA.

- Library Sales2 has an explicit grant for DeptB. Which

statement is true?

A. Mary can see Library Sales2.
B. Mary cannot see Library Sales2.
C. Mary can see Library Sales2 for data associated with DeptB only.
D. Mary can see Library Sales2 for data flagged as PUBLIC only.

QUESTION 12

In order of precedence from highest to lowest, how are permissions on a metadata item evaluated?

A. Directly applied and ACT applied, Inherited from parent, Inherited from default ACT

B. ACT applied, Directly applied, Inherited from parent, Inherited from default ACT

C. Inherited from parent, Inherited from default ACT, ACT applied, Directly applied

D. Directly applied, Inherited from parent, ACT applied, Inherited from default ACT

QUESTION 13

The WriteMemberMetadata (WWM) permission is only found on which type of items?

A. Data libraries
B. Folders
C. Information Maps
D. Data sets

QUESTION 14

Which statement regarding precedence principles for authorization is FALSE?

A. Settings on an item have priority over settings on the item's parent.
B. If identity precedence and the type of setting do not resolve a conflict, the outcome is a denial.
C. Explicit settings have priority over ACT settings.
D. A direct member of multiple groups cannot have conflicting settings.

QUESTION 15

A platform administrator needs to register OLAP cubes. What permission levels are required for this task?

A. CM for the target folder and WMMfor the OLAP schema.
B. WMfor the OLAP schema and RMLE for the target folder.
C. WM for the target folder and WMMfor the OLAP schema.
D. WM for the OLAP schema and WMMfor the target folder.

QUESTION 16

An internal account is used to provide the initial connection to which server?

A. workspace server
B. stored process server
C. SAS/SHARE server
D. metadata server

QUESTION 17

Which statement is FALSE?

Updating table metadata enables you to:

A. add table metadata for tables that exist in the physical library but have no metadata in the repository.
B. update table definitions to match corresponding physical tables.
C. update table security settings at the metadata and operating system level.
D. delete metadata for table definitions that exist in the metadata repository but do not have a corresponding table in the physical library.

QUESTION 18

A client wants to have their system set up so that stored processes can access libraries without having to manage library assignments in the stored process code. How should the libraries be assigned?

A. by default
B. by client application
C. by pre-assignment
D. by user access

QUESTION 19

The METALIB procedure enables you to update table metadata. Which method does NOT provide access to the METALIB procedure?

A. SAS Management Console's update metadata feature
B. SAS Enterprise Guide Explorer's library management feature
C. SAS Data Integration Studio's update table metadata feature
D. custom code using PROC METALIB.

QUESTION 20

When you use a connection profile and the SASSEC_LOCAL_PW_SAVE option is set to Y, which pieces of information is it possible to save?

A. User ID
B. Password
C. User ID and Password
D. No information can be saved

QUESTION 21

Which statement regarding default groups is true?

A. SASUSERS is a subset of PUBLIC
B. PUBLIC is a subset of SASUSERS
C. SASUSERS is a subset of ADMINISTRATORS
D. ADMINISTRATORS is a subset of Unrestricted Users

QUESTION 22

Given the following authorization setup:

- Mary is a direct member of DeptA.

- DeptA is a direct member of DeptB.

- Library Sales2 has an explicit denial for DeptA.

- Library Sales2 has an explicit grant for DeptB. Which

statement is true?

A.   Mary can see Library Sales2.
B.   Mary cannot see Library Sales2.
C.   Mary can see Library Sales2 for data associated with DeptB only.
D.   Mary can see Library Sales2 for data flagged as PUBLIC only.

QUESTION 23

A platform administrator needs to delete metadata for table definitions with the following characteristics:

- the table definitions exist in the metadata repository

- the table definitions do not have a corresponding table in the physical library

After performing impact analysis, what action should the platform administrator take?

A.   delete repository
B.   delete physical library
C.   delete the table's metadata folder
D.   update table metadata

QUESTION 24

Given the following applications:

- SAS Add-in for Microsoft Office

- SAS Enterprise Guide By default,

How do these applications assign libraries?

A. by using the SAS/ACCESS interface
B. by using the metadata LIBNAME engine
C. by using the BASE SAS engine
D. by using the server autoexec file

QUESTION 25

A customer's environment has a standard workspace server instantiated by the object spawner. What authentication is required to support this configuration?

A. back-end authentication
B. integrated authentication
C. host authentication
D. internal authentication

QUESTION 26

Which permissions are found on all metadata item types?

A. RM WM RMM RW Administer
B. RM WM RW Administer
C. RM WM Administer
D. RM WM

QUESTION 27

A platform administrator needs to associate a library with an application server. What permission level on the application server will the platform administrator need for this task?

A. CM
B. RMLE
C. WM
D. WMM

QUESTION 28

Given the following authorization setup:
- Mary is a direct member of DeptA and DeptB
- Library Sales2 has an explicit RM denial for DeptA.

- Library Sales2 has an explicit RM grant for DeptB. Which

statement is true?

A. Mary can see Library Sales2.
B. Mary cannot see Library Sales2.
C. Mary can see Library Sales2 for data associated with DeptB only.
D. Mary can see Library Sales2 for data flagged as PUBLIC only.

QUESTION 29

What is the correct order in which to start up the SAS servers and spawners?

A. Batch server, metadata server, object spawner, OLAP server, pooled workspace server, stored process server, workspace server

B. Workspace server, stored process server, pooled workspace server, OLAP server, object spawner, metadata server, batch server

C. Metadata server, batch server, object spawner, OLAP server, pooled workspace server, stored process server, workspace server

D. Metadata server, object spawner, OLAP server

QUESTION 30

A platform administrator wants to physically segregate the physical storage for metadata in a single environment. What should the platform administrator create?

A. additional foundation repositories
B. additional custom repositories
C. additional project repositories
D. additional repository libraries

QUESTION 31

A user needs to modify metadata. Which method should be used?

A.   Use the appropriate SAS application to make the modification.

B.   Open the SAS data sets where the metadata is stored and make the modification.

C.   Move the files to a project repository and open the SAS data sets in the physical folder to make the modification.

D.   Use SAS Management Console's Metadata Manager plug-in to make the modification.

QUESTION 32

You used the SAS Add-In for Microsoft Office in Microsoft Excel to view a SAS OLAP cube. Which type of server is used to access the OLAP cube?

A.   OLAP server
B.   Workspace server
C.   OLAP and workspace server
D.   OLAP and batch server

QUESTION 33

If a server or spawner is failing to start, what would be the most appropriate first step in troubleshooting the cause of the failure?

A. Run the SAS Deployment Manager to reconfigure the servers.

B. Modify the SAS Server configuration files.

C. Copy the command line used to invoke the server and issue it directly in the operating system, noting any errors or information generated.

D. Use SAS Management Console to modify the server's configuration.

QUESTION 34

Metadata repositories are a collection of files in a physical folder. In what format are the files stored?

A. SAS data sets

B. SAS metadata sets

C. XML

D. SGML

QUESTION 35

By default, the SASMeta application server context:

A. can only be accessed by unrestricted users.
B. is a backup for the SASApp application server context.
C. only holds the metadata server definition.
D. holds the metadata server definition and a definition for a workspace server and DATA step batch server used for administrative functions.

QUESTION 36

Which groups are pre-defined in the SAS metadata?

A. SASUSERS
B. SAS Administrators
C. SAS General Servers
D. All of the above

QUESTION 37

The SAS configuration directory on each server machine must be protected by:

A. metadata access controls.
B. operating system controls.
C. the Authorization Manager of SAS Management Console.
D. the default Access Control Template (ACT) .

QUESTION 38

Identify the object type that can be promoted.

A. users
B. ACT's
C. roles
D. libraries

QUESTION 39

Your environment contains a restore program named restoreServer.sas. Which statement regarding restoreServer.sas is FALSE?

A. It connects to the metadata server using the SAS Trust credentials.
B. It writes a log to the metadata server directory.
C. You can execute the program in a SAS session with XCMD option enabled.
D. It restores the backup files from the SASBackup directory to the appropriate subdirectories in the metadata server directory.

QUESTION 40

Which statement is FALSE regarding the use of the OMABAKUP macro to backup the SAS environment?

A. It can be used to restore the backup files.
B. It can be used to reclaim unused disk space with the REORG option.
C. It stops the metadata server while performing a backup.
D. It creates a backup with minimal disruption in service.

QUESTION 41

A host is using an LDAP provider as a back-end authentication mechanism. For this setup, how does the SAS server view the authentication?

A. integrated authentication
B. back-end authentication
C. internal authentication
D. host authentication

QUESTION 42

By default, which type of servers run under shared credentials?

A. Stored process server and workspace server
B. Workspace server and pooled workspace server
C. Pooled workspace server and stored process server
D. Stored process server, workspace server, and pooled workspace server

QUESTION 43

Identify the repository that holds information about the other repositories in the environment.

A. custom repository
B. foundation repository
C. project repository
D. repository manager

QUESTION 44

The passwords for service accounts that occur in some of the configuration files have been changed. What action should the platform administrator take?

A. Directly edit passwords in the configuration files.
B. Update passwords with the SAS Management Console.
C. Update passwords directly in the metadata with the Proc Metadata procedure.
D. Update passwords with the SAS Deployment Manager.

QUESTION 45

If you are unable to connect to or use a server, which of the following would NOT be a viable first step in troubleshooting?

A. Verify that the server is running at the operating system level.
B. Modify the SAS Server configuration files and attempt to restart.
C. Verify that the object spawner is running at the operating system level for the workspace and stored process servers.
D. Examine logs to identify warnings or errors.

QUESTION 46

How many object spawners, at a minimum, need to be defined in the metadata?

A. One per machine running a stored process server, workspace server, and/or pooled workspace server.

B. One for each type of server instantiated by an object spawner.

C. One for every three servers that need to be instantiated by an object spawner.

D. Never more than one per environment.

QUESTION 47

In what state must the metadata server be in if you choose to use operating system commands to backup metadata repositories?

A. Online
B. Running
C. Administration
D. Stopped

QUESTION 48

Which statement is a disadvantage of pre-assigned libraries?

A.   The server does not become available to the user until all pre-assigned libraries have been assigned.

B.   Pre-assigned libraries must be identical across all SAS client applications.

C.   Pre-assigned libraries must be assigned using the autoexec file.

D.   The administrator cannot control which engine is used to access data in a pre-assigned library.

QUESTION 49

Select the method for updating table metadata that provides for the most control over updating features and can be run in batch.

A.   Update Metadata option in Data Library Manager in SAS Management Console.

B.   Update Library Metadata task in SAS Enterprise Guide.

C.   Update Metadata option in SAS Data Integration Studio.

D.   METALIB procedure using SAS code.

QUESTION 50

For metadata library connections to an RDBMS, which statement is true?

A.   Security is only applied if the library is pre-assigned.

B.   Security can be applied only in the RDBMS.

C.   Security can be applied only in SAS metadata.

D.   Security can be applied in SAS metadata and in the RDBMS.

QUESTION 51

A platform administrator wants to prevent all restricted users from accessing data that requires the Read permission. Which permission level(s) should the platform administrator assign?

A. RM and R for PUBLIC
B. RM and R for PUBLIC and SAS Administrators
C. R for PUBLIC
D. RM for PUBLIC and SAS System Services

QUESTION 52

A platform administrator wants to provide SAS Administrators and service identities with exclusive read access to metadata. Which permission levels should the platform administrator assign?

A. RM for PUBLIC, SAS Administrators, and SAS System Services
B. RM and R for PUBLIC, SAS Administrators, and SAS System Services
C. RM for PUBLIC, and R for SAS Administrators and SAS System Services
D. R for PUBLIC, and RM for SAS Administrators and SAS System Services

QUESTION 53

An identity hierarchy specifies a list of identities and the order of precedence of those identities. Which listing of identities is ranked from highest priority to lowest priority?

A. User, direct group, indirect group, SASUSERS, PUBLIC
B. User, SASUSERS, PUBLIC, direct group, indirect group
C. SASUSERS, PUBLIC, User, direct group, indirect group
D. direct group, indirect group, User, PUBLIC, SASUSERS

QUESTION 54

You have used the SAS Management Console to unregister a repository. Which statement is true?

A. The metadata and physical files for the repository are deleted.
B. The metadata for the repository is deleted but the physical files are not affected.
C. The metadata for the repository is not affected but the physical files are deleted.
D. The metadata and physical files for the repository are not affected.

QUESTION 55

You have used the SAS Management Console to delete a repository. Which statement is true?

A.   The metadata and physical files for the repository are deleted.

B.   The metadata for the repository is deleted but the physical files are not affected.

C.   The metadata for the repository is not affected but the physical files are deleted.

D.   The metadata and physical files for the repository are not affected.

QUESTION 56

After the SAS configuration completes, all of the configuration directories, files, and scripts are owned by:

A.   the user who performed the installation.

B.   the SAS Platform Administrator.

C.   the SAS Data Integration Developer.

D.   the site's IT manager.

QUESTION 57

A platform administrator used operating system commands to backup the metadata repositories and repository manager in a SAS environment. When the platform administrator attempted to restore the SAS environment, the backup files were unusable. What is the most likely cause of the backup files being unusable?

A. The metadata server was stopped when the backup was taken.

B. The metadata server was Online when the backup was taken.

C. The metadata server was only paused to an Offline state when the backup was taken.

D. The metadata server configuration file omaconfig.xml is not included in a backup initiated by operating system commands.

QUESTION 58

A platform administrator needs to restore backup files to a running metadata server. Which macro can the platform administrator use to perform this task?

A. OMAREORG
B. OMARESTORE
C. OMACONFIG
D. OMABAKUP

QUESTION 59

The metadata server is stopped. What will be the result when operating system commands are used to backup the metadata repositories and repository manager?

A.   The backup files will be unusable.
B.   The backup files will not include metadata configuration files.
C.   The backup files should be usable for a restore.
D.   The backup files will include metadata configuration files only.

QUESTION 60

Which of the following is NOT a method you could use to restore your SAS environment?

A.   Use the restore job created by the Backup Wizard.
B.   Execute the restoreServer.sas program.
C.   Write custom code to invoke the OMABAKUP macro with the RESTORE option enabled.
D.   Use the RESTORE macro.

QUESTION 61

To support seamless access to database servers or SAS processing servers, a login for outbound use may be defined in the metadata. An outbound login must include:

A.   a user ID.
B.   a user ID and password.
C.   a user ID and authentication domain.
D.   a user ID, password, and authentication domain.

QUESTION 62

Given the definition: A SAS metadata object that pairs logins with the server definitions where those credentials will correctly authenticate. What is being defined?

A. authentication domain
B. outbound login
C. cached credential
D. retrieved credential login

QUESTION 63

A platform administrator needs to provide seamless access to the standard workspace server in a mixed provider environment. SAS Token Authentication is not applicable. How should the platform administrator handle passwords for external accounts?

A. Store the passwords in the metadata.
B. Store the passwords in an external file.
C. Assign the passwords to an authentication domain.
D. Store the passwords in a SAS internal account.

QUESTION 64

A platform administrator has converted the standard workspace server to use SAS Token Authentication in a mixed provider environment. What will be the outcome of this conversion?

A. Credential caching will be used to provide access.

B. Windows and Unix servers will have aligned authentication providers.

C. Host access by individual accounts will be provided.

D. Seamless access will be provided.

QUESTION 65

Which statement is an advantage of pre-assigned libraries?

A. Libraries are available in stored processes with no additional steps.

B. Metadata security is always applied to pre-assigned libraries.

C. User-written formats are only available to pre-assigned libraries.

D. Maintenance is reduced for the platform administrator.

Answers

1. Correct Answer: A
2. Correct Answer: C
3. Correct Answer: C
4. Correct Answer: C
5. Correct Answer: D
6. Correct Answer: B
7. Correct Answer: C
8. Correct Answer: D
9. Correct Answer: A
10. Correct Answer: B
11. Correct Answer: A
12. Correct Answer: A
13. Correct Answer: B
14. Correct Answer: D
15. Correct Answer: D
16. Correct Answer: D
17. Correct Answer: C
18. Correct Answer: C
19. Correct Answer: B
20. Correct Answer: C
21. Correct Answer: A
22. Correct Answer: B
23. Correct Answer: D
24. Correct Answer: B

25.   Correct Answer: C
26.   Correct Answer: D
27.   Correct Answer: C
28.   Correct Answer: B
29.   Correct Answer: D
30.   Correct Answer: B
31.   Correct Answer: A
32.   Correct Answer: A
33.   Correct Answer: C
34.   Correct Answer: A
35.   Correct Answer: D
36.   Correct Answer: D
37.   Correct Answer: B
38.   Correct Answer: D
39.   Correct Answer: A
40.   Correct Answer: C
41.   Correct Answer: D
42.   Correct Answer: C
43.   Correct Answer: D
44.   Correct Answer: D
45.   Correct Answer: B
46.   Correct Answer: A
47.   Correct Answer: D
48.   Correct Answer: B
49.   Correct Answer: D
50.   Correct Answer: D
51.   Correct Answer: C

52. Correct Answer: A
53. Correct Answer: A
54. Correct Answer: B
55. Correct Answer: A
56. Correct Answer: A
57. Correct Answer: B
58. Correct Answer: D
59. Correct Answer: C
60. Correct Answer: D
61. Correct Answer: D
62. Correct Answer: A
63. Correct Answer: A
64. Correct Answer: D
65. Correct Answer: A

www.ingramcontent.com/pod-product-compliance
Lightning Source LLC
LaVergne TN
LVHW022126060326
832903LV00063B/4760